THE SEA SKATER

HELEN DUNMORE

The Sea Skater

BLOODAXE BOOKS

ISBN: 1 85224 006 7

First published 1986 by
Bloodaxe Books Ltd,
P.O. Box 1SN,
Newcastle upon Tyne NE99 1SN.

This book is published with
the financial support of South West Arts

WITH THE ASSISTANCE OF

SOUTH WEST ARTS

Bloodaxe Books Ltd acknowledges
the financial assistance of Northern Arts.

Typesetting by Bryan Williamson, Swinton, Berwickshire.

Printed in Great Britain by
Tyneside Free Press Workshop Ltd, Newcastle upon Tyne.

For Francis, Ollie & Patrick

Acknowledgements

Acknowledgements are due to the editors of the following magazines in which some of these poems first appeared: *Encounter*, *The Literary Review*, *Other Poetry*, *Poetry Durham*, *Poetry Wales*, *South West Review*, *Spare Rib*, *Stand*, and *Writing Women*. 'Porpoise washed up on the beach' was published in the anthology *South West Review: A Celebration*, edited by Lawrence Sail (South West Arts, 1985). 'In the tea house' was broadcast on *Poetry Now* (BBC Radio 3).

'The sea skater' and 'The horse landscape' won prizes in the Poetry Society's National Poetry Competition in 1984 and 1985, and were broadcast on BBC Radio 3.

Contents

The bride's nights in a strange village

At three in the morning
while mist limps between houses
while cloaks and blankets
dampen with dew

the bride sleeps with her husband
bundled in a red blanket,
her mouth parts and a bubble
of sour breathing goes free.
She humps wool up to her ears
while her husband tightens his arms
and rocks her, mumbling. Neither awakes.

In the second month of the marriage
the bride wakes after midnight.
Damp-bodied
she lunges from sleep
hair pricking with sweat
breath knocking her sides.
She eels from her husband's grip
and crouches, listening.

The night is enlarged by sounds.
The rain has started.
It threshes leaves secretively
and there in the blackness
of whining dogs it finds out the house.
Its hiss enfolds her, blots up
her skin, then sifts off, whispering
in her like mirrors
the length of the rainy village.

Lazarus

Dumb, his lips swathed,
lips peaceful and dry

out of the swash and backwash of speech,

his face bound with a napkin,
his arms and his legs with gravecloths
in glistening daylight,

in dumbness, silky as flints
packed into chalk cliffs.

The age of the iron man
finished, the age of the stone
still blooming. Here are the avenues,
peaceful avenues with stone petals.

Here is a red-veined marble, and there
the white Carrara with black tracing

and all the messages, the pollen
on which passers-by hang, bee-like,

words joined onto words.

Dumb, his lips sealed
with mouth-to-mouth breathing,

he abhors earth music:
the midday, dwindling
shadow of requiems.

A life-size statue of limestone,
scaly and worn over nostril
and lip-arches,

with yellow lichen and snails
poured into his eyes.

Liquid oboe pulsations
trail him, but dumbly
he pedals his stone body onward

past slab after word-covered slab
towards the expressionless sea he loves best,

to Bethsaida from Bethany.

Christmas roses

I remember years ago, that we had Christmas roses:
cold, greeny things under the snow –
fantastic hellebores, harbingers
of the century's worst winter.

On little fields stitched over with drystone
we broke snow curds, our sledge
tossing us out at the wall.

For twelve years a plateau of sea
stopped at my parents' window.
Here the slow Flatholm foghorn
sucking at the house fabric

recalls my little month-old brother,
kept in the house for weeks
while those snow days piled up like plates
to an impossible tower.

They were building the match factory
to serve moors seeded with conifers
that year of the Bay of Pigs,

the year of Cuba, when adults muttered
of taking to the moors with a shotgun
when the bomb dropped.

Such conversation, rapaciously
stored in a nine year old's memory
breeds when I stare down Bridgwater Bay
to that glassy CEGB elegance, Hinkley
Point, treating the landscape like snow,
melting down marshes and long, lost
muddy horizons.

Fir thickets replace those cushions
of scratchy heather, and prick out the noise
of larks in the air, so constant
I never knew what it was.

Little hellebores with green veins,
not at all tender, and scentless
on frosty ground, with your own small
melt, your engine of growth:
that was the way I liked you.

I imagine you sent back from Africa

I imagine you sent back from Africa
leaving a patchwork of rust and khaki
sand silt in your tea and your blood.

The metal of tanks and cans
puckers your taste-buds.
Your tongue jumps from the touch
of charge left in a dying battery.

You spread your cards in the shade
of roving lorries whose canvas
tents twenty soldiers.
The greased cards patter
in chosen spaces.

I imagine you sent back from Africa
with a tin mug kept for the bullet hole
in at one angle and out another.

You mount the train at the port
asking if anywhere on earth
offers such grey, mild people.

Someone draws down the blind.
You see his buttons, his wrist,
his teeth filled to the roots.
He weakens the sunlight for you
and keeps watch on your face.
Your day sinks in a hollow of sleep
racket and megaphoned voices.

The troop-ship booms once. Laden
with new men she moves down the Sound
low in the water, egg-carrying.

But for you daylight
with your relieved breath
supping up train dirt.
A jolt is a rescue from sleep
and a glaze of filth from the arm-rest
patches your cheek. You try to catch voices
calling out stations closer to home.

The knight

In the dusk of a forest chapel
a knight lies bleeding.

The edges of his wound are rawly
exhausted by blood chafing
but still the blood gathers and wells.

At first he lay with his arms folded
waiting for his brother officers
his dog curled at his feet,

but soon the dog with a whimper
made off, tearing its fur,
and soon the knight, moaning,
tried to cuddle into a foetal position
but the terrible wound prevented him.

His armour has become a bandage
as stiff as the casing of a chrysalis.
His face no longer has the strength for amazement.

The knight cries for his mother
in the dark of a forest chapel.
He wants the smell of her
and of all living things
which are not bleeding.

The scent and hissing of pine needles
make him believe he's in a hospital
where nurses pass by him.
He is afraid of falling
and of the stone floor under him.

In the dusk of a forest chapel
a knight lies bleeding.
In search of comfort
he turns to the warmer
grain of the wooden
bench he lies on
and licks its salty
whorls with his tongue.

In memoriam Cyril Smith 1913-1945

I've approached him since childhood,
since he was old, blurred,

my stake in the playground chants
and war games,

a word like 'brother'
mixed with a death story.

Wearing shorts and a smile
he stayed in the photograph box.

His hair was receding early.
He had Grandpa's long lip and my mother's love.

The jungle obliterates a city
of cries and murmurs,
bloody discharges
and unsent telegrams.

Now he is immanent

breaking off thoughts

printing that roll of film
one sweaty evening.

Four decades
have raised a thicket of deaths around him

a fence of thorn and a fence of roses.

His mother, my grandmother,
his father, his brother,

his camp companions

his one postcard.

The circle closes
in skin, limbs
and new resemblances.

We wanted to bring him
through life with us

but he grows younger.

We've passed him
holding out arms.

The parachute packers

The parachute packers with white faces
swathed over with sleep
and the stale bodily smell of sheets

make haste to tin huts where a twelve-hour
shift starts in ten minutes.
Their bare legs pump bicycle pedals,
they clatter on wooden-soled sandals
into the dazzling light over the work benches.

They rub in today's issue of hand-cream.
Their fingers skim on the silk
as the unwieldy billows of parachute flatten
like sea-waves, oiled, folded in sevens.

The only silk to be had
comes in a military packaging:
dull-green, printed, discreet,
gone into fashioning parachutes
to be wondered at like the flowers'
down-spinning, seed-bearing canopies
lodged in the silt of village memory.

A girl pulling swedes in a field
senses the shadow of parachutes
and gapes up, knees braced
and hair tangling. She must be riddled,
her warm juices all spilled
for looking upwards too early
into the dawn, leafy with parachutes.

Heavenly wide canopies
bring down stolid chaps with their rifle butts
ready to crack, with papers
to govern the upturned land,
with boots, barbed wire and lists on fine paper
thousands of names long.

I look up now at two seagulls,
at cloud drifts and a lamp-post
bent like a feeding swan,

and at the sound of needles
seaming up parachutes in Nissen huts
with a hiss and pull through the stuff
of these celestial ball-dresses

for nuns, agents, snow-on-the-boots men
sewn into a flower's corolla
to the music of Workers' Playtime.

At dusk the parachute packers
release their hair from its nets
and ride down lanes whitened by cow-parsley
to village halls, where the dances
and beer and the first cigarettes
expunge the clouds of parachute silk
and rules touching their hair and flesh.

In the bar they're the girls who pack parachutes
for our boys. They can forget
the coughs of the guard on duty,
the boredom and long hours
and half-heard cries of caught parachutists.

Porpoise washed up on the beach

After midday the great lazy
slaps of the sea,
the whistling of a boy who likes the empty
hour while the beach is feeding,

the cliffs vacant, gulls untidily drowsing
far out on the water.

I walked on in the dazzle
round to the next cove
where the sea was running backwards like mercury
from people busy at cutting
windows in the side of a beached porpoise.

The creature had died recently.
Naturally its blood was mammalian,
its skin supple and tough; it made me
instantly think of uses for it –
shoe soling, sealing the hulls of boats –
something to explain the intent knives
and people swiftly looking at me.

But there was no mussel harvest on the rocks
or boat blinding through noon
out to the crab pots,
not here but elsewhere the settled
stupor of digestion went on.

The porpoise had brought the boys between fourteen and eighteen,
lengthened their lives by a burning
profitless noon-time,
so they cut windows out of surprise
or idleness, finding the thing here
like a blank wall, inviting them.

They jumped from its body, prodded it,
looked in its mouth and its eyes,
hauled up its tail like a child's drawing
and became serious.

Each had the use of the knife in turn
and paused over the usual graffiti
to test words first with a knife-point
and fit the grey boulder of flesh under them.

Clapping their wings the gulls came back from the sea,
the pink screens of the hotel opened,
the last boy scoured the knife with sand.

I walked back along the shingle
breathing away the bloody trail of the porpoise
and saw the boys' wet heads glittering,
their hooting, diving
bodies sweeping them out of the bay.

In deep water

For three years I've been wary of deep water.
I busied myself on the shore
towelling, handing out underwear,
wading the baby knee-high.

I didn't think I had forgotten
how to play in the deep water,
but it was only today I went there
passing the paddle boats and bathers,
the parallel harbour wall,
until there was no one at all but me
rolling through the cold water
and scarcely bothering to swim
from pure buoyancy.

Of course I could still see them:
the red and the orange armbands,
the man smiling and pointing seawards,
the tender faces.

It's these faces that have taken me
out of the deep water
and made my face clench like my mother's
once, as I pranced on a ten-foot
wall over a glass-house.

The water remembers my body,
stretched and paler as it is.
Down there is my old reflection
spread-eagled, steadily moving.

The marsh and sea-wall

The marsh and sea-wall
sundered by green
light sunk into them
are banked by the same ancestors:

whistling of sharp grasses,
old besiegings and pitiless
whirling of children's bodies,
a soft ash-pile,
unjointed elbows,

hunger for greasy wool and shoe-leather.
The cotton-grass blows and dances,
hollows are lit cups,
salt-streaks race on the marsh body.

The crackle of huts lives on by firelight.
Saxons with white plaits
are sucked back by the wet
wide mouth of the bog,
their locked bodies
mothering gas
whisper and sip travellers' lights at evening.

The sea-wall's ribbed stones
glitter like light-houses.
The mounting sea
is eager for earthliness.

The marsh and sea-wall
cling to each other,
feed, offer and breach
their mingled juices.

Salt rests on the peat
which remains breastless,
flat and liquid as sleep,
unmotherly, bone-chaste.

The big tide

At four o'clock on the beach
the heatwave day's blare peaked
over its conquests.

The water edge brimmed with children
the waves with surf riders
the deep with indefatigable
crawl swimmers flashing
spray over wet heads.

Brown headlands, ribbons of current,
purple and turquoise waters
clear as a flask
all shivered and dazzled.

The big tide came pushing through sunlight.
First one
pulse swallowed the waterside dancers
and tugged them upright, wriggling, sealed
in six feet of translucence,

the second swelled over the beach mats,
picnics, dinghies, the folded buggies
stowed by the rocks,

lipped the steps to the car park
till all music and voices went dumb,
pinned by the weight of water.

The sea leapt seven flights to the tower
and roof gardens of the Atlantic hotel
and there it crystallised flowers
and set tree trunks to marble.

The beach tumbled its creatures
like rare fruits glowing through jelly.
Some were engulfed while still sunbathing,
ecstatic eyes turned upward to salt water.

Others with skirts tucked up paddled a child
barnacled over with curls.

Some quarrelled, feeling the heat,
and drowned with irritable gestures.
Others crouched over rock pool,
teasing out sea anemones.

The sea lies flat in the sunlight,
knocking up lion-coloured cliff tops
miles over the slimes of low tide
and the evening walkers.

On the Fire Hills

A small flame scratches the tinder.
Blue-edged, wan, it spurts and collapses
as the underlying air catches it.

Cupped by a circle of hands
the flame gathers. The man jerks back
as an unreeling tongue of fire
leaps and bows down
and flares south, fanning the ground.

The cluster of watchers breaks and races
around the fire to contain it
with beating branches. They stamp out sparks
and hold the blaze to a circle,
pure, yellow, kicking for air
like a new baby.

The stars' glare smudges above them.
The moon closes upon them
and sails the path of the Fire Hills
drawing up dew and tides.
They pile up brushwood to dim her
in lolloping flames.

On the next fire hill
a watcher sets light to the gorse.
All shout and holler
to see the distance glow out, answering
their first beacon.

Three times they blanket the fire
and let it unpeel to heaven
where gods, tickled by sacrifice
humour the wits of their earth children.

The beacon rises and roars
off the Fire Hills.
It swallows sweet-smelling
turf of field scabious and harebell
and rest-harrow.
It splits the exposed chalk
and flints like buried bone rise to the surface,
cool and ready for use.

Lady Macduff and the primroses

Now the snowdrop, the wood-anemone, the crocus
have flowered
and faded back to dry, scarcely-seen threads,

Lady Macduff goes down to the meadow
where primrose flowers are thickening.

Her maid told her this morning, It's time
to pick them now, there will never be more
without some dying.

Even the kitchen girls, spared for an hour,
come to pick flowers for wine.

The children's nurse has never seemed to grasp
that she only need lay down the flowers loosely,

the flat-bottomed baskets soon fill
with yellow, chill primroses covered by sturdy leaves,

but the nurse will weave posies
even though the children are impatient
and only care who is first, has most
of their mother's quick smile.

Pasties have been brought from the castle.
Savoury juices spill from their ornate crusts,
white cloths are smeared with venison gravy
and all eat hungrily
out in the spring wind.

Lady Macduff looks round at the sparkling
sharpness of grass, whipped kerchiefs and castle battlements
edged with green light

and the primroses like a fall
colder than rain, warmer than snow,
petals quite still, hairy stems helplessly curling.

She thinks how they will be drunk
as yellow wine, swallow by swallow
filling the pauses of mid-winter,
sweet to raw throats.

Princess Charlotte

In the ante-room all evening there's Baron Stockmar
pacing, angrily breaking a pen.
Then at eleven he kneels on the carpet
and utters German baby words to the dear Princess,
stops, stares at the clock
with hatred, rings for a chop
and leaves the brown congealed mess cold in its dish.

In the bedroom Sir Richard Croft
uses his instruments to bleed her and then
muffles his forceps in cloth: does nothing. The baby
beats out its last six hours of being
against its mother's perineum.

The day quietens and darkens
(afterbirth tidied, haemorrhage lightened with water),
it comes to its end.

Charlotte repeatedly vomits. The Baron Stockmar
runs to the bell, yells for fresh bowls
and then goes in to her.
Charlotte gazes at him without speaking
then smiles and attempts to tell him
that the doctors are trying to make her drunk
– dear Stockmar!

Stockmar later found it impossible
not to believe his dead Princess
could have borne less;

Croft, possibly also believing this
after the evidence of death
fell into his own post-natal depression.
Perhaps he dreamed of the nine-pound baby
rising up for air like a diver,
or of the Princess' joke
when he fed her with wine and laudanum
while helpless blood broke through the mattress.

Mary Shelley

'No living poet ever arrived at the fulness of his
fame; the jury which sits in judgement upon a poet,
belonging as he does to all time, must be composed
of his peers.' (Percy Bysshe Shelley)

In the weightlessness of time and our passage within it
voices and rooms swim.
Cleft after soft cleft
parts, word-covered lips
thin as they speak.

I should recall how pink and tender
your lids looked when you read too long
while I produced seamed
patchwork, my own phantom.

Am I the jury, the evidence,
the recollection?

Last night I dreamed of a prospect
and so I dreamed backwards:

first I woke in the dark
scraping my knuckles on board and mould.

I remember half listening
or reading in the shadow of a fire;
each evening I would lie quietly
breathing the scent of my flesh till I slept.

I loved myself in my new dress.
I loved the coral stems rising from the rosebush
under my window in March.
I was intact, neat,
dressing myself each morning.

I dreamed my little baby was alive
mewing for me from somewhere in the room.
I chafed her feet and tucked her nightdress close.

Claire, Shelley and I left England.
We crossed the Channel and boasted afterwards
of soaked clothes, vomit and cloudbursts.

We went by grey houses, shutters still closed,
people warmly asleep. My eyes were dazed
wide open in abatement and vacancy.

*

> 'A bad wife is like winter in the house.'
>   (diary of Claire Clairmont, Florence 1820)

In Florence in winter grit scoured between houses;
the plaster needed replacing, the children had coughs.

I lived in a nursery which smelled of boredom and liniment.
In bed I used to dream of water crossings
by night. I looked fixedly forward.
It was the first winter I became ugly:
I was unloving all winter,
frozen by my own omens.

In Lerici I watched small boats on the bay
trace their insect trails on the flat water.
Orange lamps and orange blossom
lit and suffused the night garden.

Canvas slashed in a squall.
Stifling tangles of sail and fragile
masts snapping brought the boat over.
The blackened sea
kept its waves still, then tilting
knocked you into its cold crevices.

I was pressed to a pinpoint,
my breath flat.
Scarcely pulsating
I gave out nothing.

I gave out nothing before your death.
We would pass in the house with blind-lipped
anger in me.
You put me aside for the winter.

I would soften like a season
I would moisten and turn to you.
I would not conform my arms to the shapes of dead children.

I patched my babies and fed them
but death got at them.
Your eyes fed everywhere.

I wonder at bodies once clustered,
at delicate tissue
emerging unable to ripen.

Each time I returned to life
calmer than the blood which left me
weightless as the ticking of a blind-cord.
Inside my amply-filled dress
I am renewed seamlessly.

Fledged in my widow's weeds
I was made over, for this
prickle of live flesh
wedged in its own corpulence.

The plum tree

The plum was my parents' tree,
above them
as I was at my bedroom window
wondering why they chose to walk this way quietly
under the plum tree.

My sisters and I stopped playing
as they reached up and felt for the fruit.
It lay among bunches of leaves,
oval and oozing resin
out into pearls of gum.
They bit into the plums
without once glancing
back at the house.

Some years were thin:
white mildew streaking the trunk,
fruit buckled and green,

but one April
the tree broke from its temperate blossoming
and by late summer the branches
trailed earth, heavy with pound
after pound of bursting Victorias,

and I remember the oblivious steps
my parents took as they went quietly
out of the house one summer evening
to stand under the plum tree.

The air-blue gown

Tonight I'm eating the past
consuming its traces,

the past is a heap
sparkling with razor blades
where patches of sweetness
deepen to compost,

woodlice fold up their legs
and roll luxuriously,

cold vegetation
rises to blood heat.

The local sea's bare
running up to the house

tufting its waves
with red seaweed
spread against a Hebridean noon.

Lightly as sandpipers marking the shoreline
boats at the jetty sprang
and rocked upon the green water.

Not much time passes, but suddenly
now when you're crumpled after a cold
I see how the scale and changes
of few words measure us.

At this time of year I remember a cuckoo's
erratic notes on a mild morning.
It lay full-fed on a cherry branch
repeating an hour of sweetness
its grey body unstirring
its lustrous eyes turning.

Talk sticks and patches
walls and the kitchen formica
while at the table outlines
seated on a thousand evenings
drain like light going out of a landscape.

The back door closes, swings shut,
drives me to place myself inside it.
In this flickering encampment
fire pours sideways
then once more stands
evenly burning.

I wake with a touch on my face
and turn sideways
butting my head into darkness.

The wind's banging diminishes. An aircraft
wanders through the upper atmosphere
bee-like, propelled by loneliness.
It searches for a fallen corolla,
its note rising and going
as it crosses the four quarters.

The city turns a seamed cheek upward,
confides itself to the sound and hazardous
construction of a journey by starlight.

I drop back soundlessly,
my lips slackened.
Headache along is my navigator,
plummeting, shedding its petals.

It's Christmas Eve.
Against my nightdress a child's foot, burning,
passes its fever through the cotton,

the tide of bells swings
and the child winces.

The bells are shamelessly
clanging, the voices
hollering churchward.

I'm eating the past tonight
tasting gardenia perfume
licking the child-like socket of an acorn
before each is consumed.

It was not Hardy who stayed there
searching for the air-blue gown.
It was the woman who once more, secretly,
tried the dress on.

Donna Juanita and the male stickleback

At dawn Donna Juanita faces her mirror.
She watches a hawk dive on her fish pond,
the dewy garden assume colour and form,
the golden carp swim for the daphnia.
A gardener whistles, swinging his can
to damp the walks of her maze.

Donna Juanita turns to the bed
and to the man sleeping.
She draws back the sheet
so that he stirs uneasily, feeling
the cooler air and himself revealed.

She walks into the garden
taking a basket of food for her fish,
and there they dart through the lilies and glide
to their habitual feeding-places,
eeling through wet stems and white-crowned
flowers which burst in the light.

Donna Juanita wishes to touch
the golden sides of her fish.
She lets her hands sink in the green pond
and weave with the water movement.
The fish nuzzle along her. They buck
their tense bodies and, mouths wide,
guzzle the crumbled egg-yolk she gives them.

Deep in the pond a male stickleback
makes his barrel-shaped nest in the silt
and glues it with his own juices.
Now, like an anxious late-marrying man
too ugly to mate easily,
he searches for females and chivvies them
into the nest with his sharp spines.

One by one they lay their burden of eggs
until the full nest rocks there, replete.

He squirts his horde over with milky semen
and settles to wait.
Now the nest shakes
in the current of passing predators
and the male stickleback guards
his hatching eggs, snapping at carp,
blindly glaring at pond debris,
duelling with dead leaves.

The fry emerge and he shelters
and chastens the teeming brood,
herding them back to safety,
letting them feed and play in the nest doorway.

After a month the young
outgrow his cherishing.
They swim off, snapping at weed,
forgetful at once of him.
Now the exhausted male stickleback
dies beside his collapsed nest
while the females of the great pond
antic and feed in its depths.

Donna Juanita gathers her wet hem
and walks the paths with a hiss of skirts
under the mulberry whose black fruits
spatter the gravel beneath them.
At her desk in the summer-house
she sets out her documents.
Long lines of her black writing
unreel with scarcely a pause.
She deploys orchards and vineyards
and chides farmers for rent.

The garden trembles with heat.
Its leaves moisten, its shadows
are brief pools.
The carp sink to the dark silt
depths of the pond, and there, veiled
by its brown clouds, torpid,
absorb the ground meat and the egg of the morning.

My sad descendants

O wintry ones, my sad descendants,
with snowdrops in your hands you join me
to celebrate these dark, short
days lacking a thread of sun.

Three is a virtuous number,
each time one fewer to love,
the number of fairy tales,
wishes, labours for love.

My sad descendants
who had no place in the sun,
hope brought you to mid-winter,
never to spring
or to the lazy benches of summer
and old bones.

My sad descendants
whose bones are a network of frost,
I carry your burn and your pallor,
your substance dwindled to drops.

I breathe you another pattern
since no breath warmed you from mine,
on the cold of the night window
I breathe you another pattern,

I make you outlive rosiness
and envied heartbeats.

Resurrection

Tomorrow I'll walk you
past limp, sweet fields of hay,

I'll shade your forehead
and cover your round arms,

we'll drink tea from a flask
while ants carry off bread crumbs.

The tide will rise in brown pleats,
the sun will bleach you and tire you,

we'll hear the scutter of a dog's claws
and the far-off whistle of its master

as midday silences the birds
and you drowse and mutter beside me.

Slowly I'll walk you uphill
under the green trees

keeping close to the wall
as fields settle below us.

Your hand will be slippery with sun-oil
you'll be too sleepy to speak,

breathless, I'll lift you
into the dark house.

Patrick at four years old on Bonfire Night

Cursing softly and letting the matches drop
too close to the firework box,
we light an oblation
to rough-scented autumnal gods,
shaggy as chrysanthemums;

and you, in your pearly maroon
waterproof suit, with your round
baby brows, stare upward and name
chrysanthemum fountain and silver fountain
and Catherine wheel: saints' names
like yours, Patrick, and you record them.
This morning, climbing up on my pillow,
you list saints' names guessed at from school.

They go off, one by one on the ritual plank:
jack-in-a-box, high-jump and Roman candle,
searching the currant bushes with gunpowder.

We stand in savoury fumes like pillars,
our coats dark, our slow-burning fuse lit,
and make our little bonfire with spits
for foil-wrapped potatoes and hot-dogs –

by your bedtime
the rough-scented autumnal gods
fuse with the saints and jack-lanterns.

The flock

The demolition ball
sways into her bedroom

like her old-fashioned
lavatory chain and handle.

Illness nuzzles her kidneys,
kind nurses
say upsidaisy at dawn.

One nurse is mad for her hair.
Its white fleece runs
off over her fingers.

The parson would swear by Jupiter
to show he's a public school man
but these old women would have him.

A black-haired deacon
vanishes behind the death curtain
cordoning the ward.

Bags and catheters struggle like ivy
on frail hosts,
yellow nutrients
drip at one end.

Her former flat is a cloud
of layered wallpaper
gaped at from double-deckers.

A bright sheep-dog
visits the unable

offering Ovaltine
and cheery memory.

Rolling away the stone

A floral old woman
rests in a crease of sun

while ten yards farther the sea
plays with its strip of nakedness:
sun-oil, beach paraphernalia,
midsummer conceptions

and roller skates whirring
off into the blue.

Her inner pockets are stuffed
with pension book, handkerchiefs
and tubes of Parma Violet
sweets for the breath.

She's captured her sea, her air,
the sun's
unchangeable glances on her.

For hours the dark, dry
cave of her memory
is rifled, broken, assailed
through its own odours

and it splashes like a fountain
shedding its hair-grips, droplets, yellow
hairs banded by grey.

This is her finger picking at mortar;
a bolted lettuce; the clatter of a low pushchair;
all her people restored in the sea air

while she sits on the bench like a pagan
drinking her way into Valhalla.

The lemon house

It's not worth keeping the treasure of lemons
close to the house.
Three bald lemons
counted and courted
from season to season
dry behind glass shields.
Their leathery foliage
dies slowly
spotted like bay leaves in a damp climate.

Their owner comes upon
plump fruit moistened with lemon dew
hidden in waxy thickets
in her night dreams of the lemon house.

She visits Italy
where boxes lined with red and white tissue
on splintered pallets
keep the gates of the grove.

She takes a skirt-full of windfall lemons.
Shamefaced, she pays for them
under the harsh gaze of the lemon grower.

Her few lemons
roll in their satinwood box.
She cuts one open
and finds pith
half as thick as the fruit,
a spurt of juice,
a sour teaspoon
of little pips.

The horse landscape

Today in a horse landscape
horses steam in the lee of thorn hedges
on soaking fields. Horses waltz
on iron poles in dank fairgrounds.

A girl in jodhpurs on Sand Bay
leads her pony over and over
jumps made of driftwood and traffic cones.

A TV blares the gabble of photofinishes.
The bookie's plastic curtain releases
punters onto tne hot street
littered with King Cone papers.

In a landscape with clouds and chalk downs
and cream houses, a horse rigid as bone
glares up at kites and haı g-gliders.

One eye's cut from the flowered turf:
a horse skull, whispering secrets
with wind-sighs like tapping on phone wires.

The group leader in beautiful boots
always on horse-back,
the mounted lady squinnying
down at the hunt intruders,
draw blood for their own horse landscape
and scorn horse-trading, letting the beasts mate
on scrubby fields, amongst catkins
and watery ditches.

Here's a rearing bronze horse
welded to man, letting his hands
stay free for banner and weapon –
mild shadow of Pushkin's nightmare.

Trained police horses sway on great hooves.
Riders avoid our faces, and gaze
down on our skull crowns
where the bone jigsaw cleaves.

Grooms whistle and urge
the sweaty beasts to endure battle.
We're always the poor infantry
backing off Mars field,
out of frame for the heroic riders
preserved in their horse landscape.

The emigrants

I.

He refuses to see
the flushed pears hanging in drops
down to the end of their branches

or that transparent sugar which seals
pastries from the town's best bakery.

He ate these twice a year or so
after a first communion,
after a wedding.

Sugar shone on his mouth,
spilled as he thrust into the dancers,
his moist lips reddened.

Later he saw the girls in shawls, distorted
by early corpulence.
Not one of the kids below decks is his.

The steamer swings lowing
through crowded waterways.

There begin to be long movements
under the criss-cross chop of water:

shudderings; cold
muscles starting to bunch.

There are twenty-five years of labour
still to uncoil from him.
His eyes flick
over the stirring forest he will chop down,
the pigs of iron
ready to tear muscle from bone.

It depends on what's wanted
in that unhandled country. Stiffly, steadily
his body presents itself.

Meanwhile the sea tenaciously
slides to this continent or that
buries the steamer
in sluices of bitter water
lets in trudge back
clambering waves like an iron-wheeled omnibus.

II.

Weasel, the acrobat of dubious alleyways,
fell not for the two or three women
who would have had him

but for the calm, fair
sister of a journeyman carpenter:
Hilde, whose wooden-tongued shoes
clacked lightly, whose eyes drifted
out to the sea and measured it.

Only Weasel with his slippery glances
failed to see what all the passengers
knew without saying:
the girl had eyes for no one
but for her brother, a block of wood
sweet-smelling to her as cedar.

Weasel, whipped in a taut
ball of his longing
licked Hilde's obstinate body
with yellow gazes.

The colours on the sea
grew flat, flatly reflected
flesh secretly seen
at night down in the steerage.

III.

So many bundles underfoot.
Everyone's pillow and mattress
made out of canvas,
webbed, lumpy
changes of clothing, the tools,
the few
precious instruments to make them
wage earners in another continent.

But nothing redundant
you'd think, until this moment
when Hilde's brother rises
up on the deck like a blond demon
magically freed, swinging a knapsack,
hollering words no one can follow
but Hilde, scooping up skirts and running behind him.

'His ruby' she shrieks, 'His ruby.'
People gaze at each other in fresh
amazement. Is it a joke?
God knows there's always been something
disruptive about this couple
– calm in itself.

But now this roaring. The girl's feet slap
out of her shoes. She gets his elbow
while hair coils slither across her shoulders.

He is quite simply bawling,
his feet apart, stock-still now, yearning
over the lost ruby.
His sister gently
conducts him downward into the dark,

while Weasel, giving a sigh
slips off. This is his opening.

IV.

The steamer isn't expansive.
Its crowdedness
promises everything, at first:
pasts, purposes, births.

But they turn out clouded, unwanted
on voyage, tied in the bundles
that are slept on but never opened.

Weasel never gets near Hilde.
Brother and sister walk down the gang-plank
in easy paces. They see New York
ripple like cloth laid out for measuring.
They don't speak of the ruby.

Weasel poises and is distinguished
for half a moment before he dives
into the wharf-side crowd and seems
to have been there forever.

The pear tree, the unpossessed
jewel of the old country
is now extinguished.
The emigrants dissolve their pasts in labour,
in blurred decades where memory is functionless.

On her three children drowned at sea while returning to England

In the middle of a wave
I see their limbs tumble,

their nearest landfall
three little yew chests
a black and grey churchyard.

They wear night bonnets and petticoats
threaded with ribbon.
Their names grow shallow with lichen.

The rip tide tears away granite gravel
and twirls the one life-boat
round on a black, oiled
table of whirlpools.

A salt, exact
fluid drip guards the electrolyte balance
inside the mother's blue veins,
then pushes her blood tide
through valves like snapdragons.

The foghorn sounds all through,
gentle as a shepherded animal
snuffing a wreck in the cold mist of morning.

Thetis

Thetis, mother of all mothers
who fear the death of their children,
held down her baby Achilles
in the dark Styx

whose waters flow fast
without ripples or wave-break,
bearing little boats of paper
with matchstick masts,
returning not even a sigh
or drenched fibre to life.

Thetis, mother of all mothers
destined to outlive their children,
took Achilles by the heel
and thrust him into the Styx

so that sealed, immortal, dark-eyed,
he'd return to his white cradle
and to his willow rattle.

She might have held him less tightly
and for a while given him
wholly to the trustworthy river
which has no eddies or backwaters
and always carries its burdens onward,
she might have left him to play
on the soft grass of the river-edge.

But through the pressure-marks of her white fingers
the baby found his way forward
towards the wound he knew best.
Even while the arrow was in the wood
and the bow gleaming with leaves
the current of the Styx
faintly suckled and started
in the little flexed ankles
pressed against Thetis' damp breasts.

In the tents

Our day off, agreed by the wind
and miry fields and unburied dead,
in the tent with first light filtering
a rosy dawn which masks rain.

The rosiness rests on our damp flesh,
on armour stacked by the tent walls,
on our captain and his lolling companion.

I go down to the sea shore
to find white pebbles for games.
I look for the island, kidding myself
I see it hump through the waves.

Back in the tent it's warm, wine-smelling,
heavy with breath.
The lamp shines on the bodies
of our captain and his companion.

These are the tented days I remember
more than the battles.
This is the smell of a herbal rub
on great Achilles.
This is the blue soap-scum on the pitcher,
and cold parcels of goat-meat,
the yawning moment
late in the evening, when I step out
and see the stars alight in their same places.

Uncle Will's telegram

She kept Uncle Will's telegram
between the sheets of her wedding-album.
Her life-long imaginary future
dazzled the moment it came.

He tried the counter-top biro
and asked the post office clerk
to check the time of arrival
for ten words in block capitals.

In the levelled-down churchyard
they posed for·the first photographs
while powdery grandmothers
whispered 'We wish you'
and came up with the word 'Happiness'.

She stood against laurel-black cherries
while the church dived into silence,
a great maritime creature
leaving without echoes.
At the lych-gate a tide-line
of white flowers remained.

In the Flowers the best man
read Uncle Will's telegram
and the guests lifted their glasses
shouting 'Io, Io Hymen!'

One Sunday

One Sunday. The kids stashing crisps
and fruit gums in a tent in the garden.

The beds are unmade and still warm.
In the kitchen the papers drift
against the thunder of the spin-drier.

All over town it's time for church-going.
Still reading, I fumble a knob
and switch off the radio organ.
We're high up here. No sound
of bells reaches the house.

My husband gets out the car
and drives his mother to church.
Our Lady of Lourdes,
an oblong brick hulk
fronted by an enamelled Virgin,

off the main road
which blinds with chromium
and four-berth caravans
in high season.

The children wonder and want
this church like a new treat.
For days Patrick will point
at churches we pass without entering.

He has an inheritance
not from my side.
A weight of masses
shaped his ancestors,
their souls spoken for:

emigrants, miners of silver
or stay-at-homes,

nuns escaping from yearly childbirth
and prolapsed mothers,
each row of dead
remembered and prayed for,

or this inheritance:
an unread testament
posted and lost
between parents and children.

The drawing lesson

The school children circle
one of themselves, their model's
stiffened position.

The violet skylight
deepends in the last lesson.
Fire doors sigh
corridors quicken with feet.

The girl on the pedestal
droops her head lower.
The click and scribble of pencils
tries to describe her

starting with easy things:
her skirt folds,
radial, shaded;
her round eyebrows.

Last week's exercise
comes between body and pages.

Now it's flowers
for half the classroom
but on this dais
a web trembles.
These spider-legged children
must make fractional
choices on line-spinning.

The wet hands –
what are they thinking of?
Whorled, webbed
with marvellous futures.

The model's hand
is warm and succulent.
She yawns behind it.
The lines vanish.

The pencil stops and steps off
stops and steps off.
Its little tap feels a way inward
through planes and dangers:
the difficult pupils.

The teacher's cool pencil
charts normal
against the brown of the girl's cheek.

He turns a child's palm upward,
reproves stickiness,
prints, oozings and blotches.

Time's up for the children.
They parcel images
score through secretive drawing
and glaze Conté
with hissing fixative.

Their plump subject
circles behind them,
points at a known
hairslide, mocks at perspective.

Rapunzel

Rapunzel
let down your hair,

let your strong hair
wind up the water you wish for.

All your life looking down
on bright tree-tops
your days go by quickly.

You read and you eat
in your white tower top
where sunlight fans through high
windows and far below you
bushes are matted with night.

With soft thumbprints
darkness muddles your pages.
The prince arrives,
whose noisy breathing
and sweat as he vaults your window-sill
draw you like wheat fields
on the enchanted horizontal.

He seeds your body with human fragments,
dandruff, nail-clippings, dust.
The detritus of new pleasures
falls on your waxed boards.

Your witch mother, sweeping them,
sorrowfully banishes the girl
who has let a prince clamber her.

For six years you wander the desert
from level to pale level.
At night you make a bunker to sleep in
near to the coyotes.

The ragged prince plays blind-man's-buff
to the sound of your voice singing
as you gather desert grasses
in hollows hidden from him.

Daily your wise mother
unpicks the walls of the tower.
Its stones are taken for sheep-folds,
your circle of hair
hidden beneath the brambles.

Bewick's swans

Ahead of us, moving through time
with a skein's precision and mystery
over the navy spaces of winter
the inter-continental migration continues.

It starts on one moment
of one season, when time ripens
down to the soft dawn chill on a feather

or the germ sprouting in winter wheat
ready to be grazed by the wild swans.

Hour by hour the birds move up the wedge
until they fly at its point, in the keen
apex, the buffet of wind.
A dark triangle of birds streams backward
and peels away and reforms like rain on glass.

Sometimes they fall almost to the white waves
then stretch their necks and call and begin
the long pull onward, leaving a swan plunged
like an untidy bundle of sheets
swept in a ship's backwash.

See them nose the long coastline
in a glide of perfected instinct.
To their preferred feeding-grounds
they are a long arrow
shot from unimaginable nowhere.
Here they are keeled, treading
the known roughness of grass tussocks.

The private swans arch out their feathers
and preen and nourish themselves.
The mild floodlights each night
and people gathered to watch
are no stranger to the swans than the prickle
of green waiting in the wheat stripes each winter.

The sea skater

A skater comes to this blue pond,
his worn Canadian skates
held by the straps.

He sits on the grass
lacing stiff boots
into a wreath of effort and breath.

He tugs at the straps and they sound
as ice does when weight troubles it
and cracks bloom around stones

creaking in quiet mid-winter
mid-afternoons: a fine time for a skater.
He knows it and gauges the sun
to see how long it will be safe to skate.

Now he hisses and spins in jumps
while powder ice clings to the air
but by trade he's a long-haul skater.

Little villages, stick-like in the cold,
offer a child or a farm-worker
going his round. These watch him
go beating onward between iced alders
seawards, and so they picture him
always smoothly facing forward, foodless and waterless,
mounting the crusted waves on his skates.

In the tea house

In the tea house the usual
customers sit with their cooling
tea glasses
and new pastries
sealed at the edge
with sticky droplets.

The waitress walks off,
calves solid and shapely as vases,
leaving a juicy baba
before her favourite.

Each table has bronze or white chrysanthemums
and the copper glass-stands imperceptibly
brush each other like crickets
suddenly focussed at dusk,

but the daily newspapers
dampened by steam
don't rustle.

The tea house still has its blinds out
even though the sun is now amiably
yellow as butter

and people hurrying by raise up their faces
without abandon, briskly
talking to their companions;

no one sits out at the tables
except a travel-stained couple
thumbing a map.

The waitress reckons her cloths
watching the proprietor
while he, dark-suited, buoyant,
pauses before a customer.

Her gaze breaks upon the tea-house
like incoming water
joining sandbanks swiftly and
softly moving the pebbles,

moving the coloured sugar and coffee
to better places,
counting the pastries.

Field study at a disused mineworking

Near to a double row of beech trees
there is a pond, sheltered and downward,
where treetrunks lie.

This is above the tunnels of a disused mineworking
faced with white, separating stones.
A sign says the buildings are dangerous.
The buildings are down, knee-high, peeled
to ruin under the grey beech-wood.

Culvert and shaft stay, pinned
tight by their dressed stone.
They swallow orange and blue anoraks.

Marsh grass covers the hurled excrescences
of earth, unwanted and hummocky,
shifting from season to season
under pattering school children
on field trips.

What is important here? The habitat?
A plastic hand has been left by one party
pointing jollily upward. Larks
throw themselves skywards, balance on fountains of air.
How many hydra
per cubic centimentre teem in that pond?
You see those beeches, the rhododendrons
budding beneath?
There was a house here.
Find out for whom the rhododendrons were planted.

Or is it mineral analysis? A view?
A long day out and lying tiredly
on bunks, laughing at Miss?
At supper there are copyright sheets
of songs once sung in the tunnels
and a release
of air as nylon haversacks flatten.

The children grow noisy on the path under the trees,
having wondered at slender disappearing shafts,
at labour and labour's abandonment.
They've peeped in tunnels they will not enter
and made maps of the silenced mineworkings.
They do a weekend's field trip, then home
still two years off school-leaving.

The rich boy

Under his dense-textured skin there are
easily scored, unmasked
particles shifting,

putting a disease together.
The clusters collide
the white knights fight

and fly off in a shower, airily
as if nothing is worth it

to a rich boy in gold harness.

There is his grandmother waiting
with veins blue as forget-me-nots.
She wants to kiss him.

There is a baby
and nurse in a linen apron
looking for madam.

A persistent shower over the cradle
makes the apartment glisten.

But the rich boy is out sailing.
Back and forth across the bay
he goes, wedged, waterproof,
shedding white teeth as he sweeps
water-skiers landwards.

A rainbow-skinned oilstain
tacks on the sea
after the outboard engine.

There is a lurch within
the rich flesh.
Something he's eaten.

The graveyard in snow

There are two of us walking away from the graveyard.
The hills are yellow and rounded, we plod
over their folds, we wear old coats
drawn warmly around us, and boots
which stick and exhaust our legs.

We are planted here in a snowfield,
our faces waxy. We hold baskets
heavy with leftover bulbs, trowels and forks.
We've lifted squares of the snow like turves
and set narcissi with our white fingers.

These cold furred lozenges, the gravestones,
we've swept only in passing
seeing ours offer a breast of snow
unmounted by stone.

A coverlet separates us.
Is that snow wind's whine the same
travelling still, the rising wind
and tide reaching your body buried in sand?

Florence in permafrost

Cold pinches the hills around Florence.
It roots out vines, truffles for lemon trees
painfully heated by charcoal
to three degrees above freezing.

A bristling fir forest
moves forward over Tuscany.
A secret wood
riddled with worm and lifeless
dust-covered branches
stings the grass and makes it flowerless,

freezing the long-closed eyelids of Romans.
They sleep entrusted to darkness
in the perpetual, placid, waveless
music of darkness.

The forest ramps over frontiers and plains
and swallows voluble Customs men
in slow ash. A wind sound
scrapes its thatching of sticks.

Blind thrushes in the wood blunder
and drop onto the brown needles.
There are no nests or singing-places.

A forest of matchwood and cheap furniture
marches in rows. Nobody harvests
its spongey woods and makes the trunks sigh
like toy soldiers giving up life.

All over Italy and northward
from fair Florence to München
and the cold city of Potsdam
the forest spreads like a pelt
on meadows, terraces, riverbanks
and the shards of brick houses.

It hides everywhere from everywhere
as each point of perspective
is gained by herds of resinous firs.

There may be human creatures
at nest in the root sockets.
They whicker words to each other
against the soughing of evergreens
while the great faces of reindeer
come grazing beside the Arno.

Geneva

City of burghers and freedom fighters,
city without hinterlands,

November burns bright
on the Rhone pouring down snow
over the city of walled-up fighters.

Next to the glassy leaders,
a statue of Zwingli,
next to the nugget of glass
in the heart, 'our country
free from the Empire'.

Bone, liver and lights
join at the sheer table.
Little cancerous atoms
burn bright.

City without hinterlands
imagining 1812
and the retreat from Moscow,

Geneva, gin-clear
city of burghers and freedom fighters,
whose army has flapped off
from the immortal mantelpiece
coated with good Genevese messages,

whose Swiss guards stand at the Holy See
holding our squeezed breath,

fill their hearts up with rain, their livers with rain,
streak their document cases with rain,

fill their borrowed households with raindrops and buckets,
sink their hearts in a river brimming with peppermint,

let washed gobbets of paper
flower in overflows,

let the scarred seams of their skins,
their ageing diseases, their birthmarks
wash them away, make rivers of them

with slow, broad drops on the hart's-tongue fern
and slow, broad drops on the wet leaves
of the city of burghers and freedom fighters –
gin-clear Geneva.

Missile launcher passing at night

The soft fields part in hedges, each
binds each, copse pleats
rib up the hillside.

Darkness is coming and grass
bends downward.
The cattle out all night
eat, knee-deep, invisible
unless a headlight arcs on their mild faces.

The night's damp fastens, droplet by droplet,
onto the animals.
They vibrate to the passing of a missile launcher
and stir
their patient eyelashes.

A blackbird
startled by floodlights
reproduces morning.

Cattle grids tremble and clang,
boots scrape
holly bursts against wet walls
lost at the moment of happening.